CHANGING THE NAME TO OCHESTER

Books by Ed Ochester

Changing the Name to Ochester
Miracle Mile
Natives (anthology)
Dancing on the Edges of Knives

Limited Editions:

Weehawken Ferry
A Drift of Swine
The End of the Ice Age
The Third Express
The Great Bourgeois Bus Company
We Like it Here

CHANGING THE NAME TO OCHESTER

poems by

Ed Ochester

Carnegie Mellon University Press
Pittsburgh 1988

Acknowledgments

Acknowledgments are due the editors of the following
magazines for first publication of many of these poems:

ANTIOCH REVIEW, CHARITON REVIEW, CINCINNATI
POETRY REVIEW, CRAZYHORSE, IMAGES, KANSAS
QUARTERLY, LIGHT YEAR 84, LIGHT YEAR 87, NEW
LETTERS, OPEN PLACES, NORTH AMERICAN REVIEW,
SOUTHERN POETRY REVIEW, VIRGINIA QUARTERLY
REVIEW, WESTERN HUMANITIES REVIEW.

"New Day," "The Relatives," and "Having Built the Coop"
first appeared in *Poetry*.

"Poem Written for the Fifth Anniversary of the Three Rivers
Shakespeare Festival" first appeared in the 1985 Festival
Program.

Thanks to John Judson and Juniper Press for printing some of
these poems in my chapbook, *Weehawken Ferry* (1985).

Most of the poems in this book were written with the assistance
of grants from the National Endowment for the Arts and The
Pennsylvania Council on the Arts. I'm grateful to those
agencies, and particularly to Peter Carnahan for his assistance
over many years.

Special thanks to poets in the Pittsburgh area whose lives and
works have energized mine: Jim Daniels, Patricia Dobler,
Bruce Dobler, Lynn Emanuel, Nancy Koerbel, Kristin Kovacic,
Frank Lehner, Peter Oresick, John Repp, Kevin Rippin, Judith
Vollmer; and to my best critic, Britt.

Publication of this book is supported by grants from the
National Endowment for the Arts in Washington, D.C., a
Federal agency, and from the Pennsylvania Council on the Arts.

Library of Congress Catalog Number 87-71455
ISBN 0-88748-068-3
ISBN 0-88748-069-1 Pbk.

Printed and bound in the United States of America
First Edition

For Frank Bachtle

1904—1987

who taught me much
of what I know
about patience
and justice

CONTENTS

I.

II.

III.

IV.

I

PACKING LUNCH

Of course I'd rather have Crab Louis
or Moules à la Provençale or Shrimp Mornay,
or Flavio's fettucini carbonara —
though what with the fresh cream and
home-cured bacon I'd be digging
my own grave with my teeth — or even
skirt steak, which Bob Watt called
a little sexy for Milwaukee, but all that
would be violating what Thoreau said
about being rich in inverse proportion
to one's needs; and besides, if I hadn't
bagged my lunch I wouldn't have gone
to Roy Rogers to buy a Diet Coke and
slip a few free tomato slices
into a napkin and heard two grad students
arguing, one saying "I'm perfectly willing
to discuss laissez-faire capitalism
in a rational way if you'd *please*
stop impugning my mother," and maybe
I wouldn't have felt free to call London
($1.76 a minute, direct dial) to say hello,
me not too far from where
Braddock in His Majesty's Service
got wiped in the French and Indian Wars
and twenty miles from where Colonel Armstrong,
"the hero of Kittanning," returned the favor
by slaughtering Delawares on Blanket Hill
which is now an abandoned speedway
covered by weeds, and if I didn't have time —
which is everything — I couldn't reread Proust,
as Reynolds Price says he's doing this summer,
because he's willing to make "the all-but-endless
concessions of time, attention, and boredom"
Proust demands, though maybe I don't want
to reread Proust, maybe I just want to dream
today about Coney Island when I was a kid,
and Steeplechase hadn't been torn down and
how you entered it through a huge rolling barrel
where almost nobody could stand up and
as the bodies slid around and on top
of one another enormous mechanical laughter and
static crackled from the loudspeakers, but it was ok,

you crawled out and stood up again and smiled,
but the only thing left of Steeplechase
is the giant Parachute Ride, dead for years
and looking like the Eiffel Tower in the midst
of Paris bombed though I remember riding
The Cyclone for the fourth time in a night
with my father who was turning green but
who told my mother "I can't let the boy
ride something as dangerous as this by himself"
so that while we rode she stood anxious, peering
up at the roller coaster cars clattering
on the rickety track all around her,
as outside the vendors sold boiled corn from
sidewalk vats, and the goony sailors alive
home from Korea walked their girls up and down
the boardwalk, singing and talking dirty and
the smells of unhealthy food everywhere —
frozen chocolate bananas, and rainbow
cotton candy and hot Italian sausage
blanketed in cheese on a bun — and later,
snacking at Nathan's Famous, the ambulances whining
past on Coney Island Avenue and the Famous
Irish Tenor singing in the bar next door,
my father told me how Luna Park had burned down
when he was a kid, and how Luna Park
(I thought: "Luna moths") made Steeplechase
look like nothing;

o love, I'm going on
because first images are clearer,
or maybe it's that in early memories
everyone is still alive, and maybe
that's what Freud misunderstood in his strictures
on "the oceanic feeling" and maybe that's why
I've already spent time today talking to Ted Weesner
who's going to that writers' conference in Maine
and is smiling about it, though they have him listed
as a poet rather than a fiction writer
which is ok, he probably should be a poet
though his movie options would be a lot less,
and why I told him how I used to spend time on the Cape
when I was 20, gathering mussels from the rocks
in the tide pools to steam with a little
white wine and parsley and basil for my friends,
some of whom are gone, and afterwards
smoke cigars and watch the breakers rolling —

"why don't you count the sand?" my mother
said once at the beach when I was six or seven —
and to tell the truth, I'm thinking *time*
a lot lately, and about what's necessary,
and even more since this morning when Dave
agreed with me about a mutual friend,
that there's no use talking about it
or devising strategies or travelling to China,
if you want to write you just sit your ass
down in a chair and begin to type, though
of course it's more than just that, it's
studying as I did last night a silver siliqua
of the Emperor Gratian, that unlucky, dead
handsome man, gone nearly 1700 years, who
was too busy and too miserable to love,
though I'm not sure what "love" means
if it doesn't have the luxury of a life's
memory, which of course is too dangerous
for any of us to ride by ourselves; and
I guess it's what I'm thinking just now,
how Hugo told me a year before he went back
on the sauce, that "it's amazing how much work
you get done when you stop drinking," and
I guess it's because he drank a bit
that I'm thinking too about Doctor Breslau,
that good man, our dentist, who ministered
to the poor and got mugged for it, and who
lent me once when I was very young
three books by Shaw — and of course because
irony is very cheap and omnipresent
Heartbreak House was one of them —
and had a collection of skulls
from digs in Mexico in his waiting room
and would happily discuss the various kinds
of dental caries manifest in each, and how
at my birth he gave my parents
a ten dollar gold piece for me,
which I sold when I was in high school
to get money for a date, so that
I have nothing left from him and
I am beginning to weep and
I am writing the first draft of this
as much as I can
on a plain brown paper bag.

II

CHANGING THE NAME TO OCHESTER

When other grandpas came to Ellis Island
the Immigration people asked "Name?"
and they said "Sergius Bronislaus Jygzywglywcz"
and the officer said "ok, from now on your name's
Sarge Jerko," and Sarge trundled off to the Lower East Side
with a lead cross and a sausage wrapped in a hair shirt
and shared a tiny ill-lit room with eight *Landleute*
and next to a pot of boiling diapers began to carve
yo-yos to peddle on the street and forty years later
was Sarge Jerko, Inc., the Yo-Yo King,
but my grandfather was born in this country
(no one living knows anything about *his* parents)
and was an engineer for Con Edison
when he married the immigrant girl
Katherina Humrich who everybody said
was once very pretty but when I knew her
had a tight bun, thin German lips
and a nose which came to her chin;
her major pleasures were trips to Coney Island
with friends and frightening little children
by jumping out from behind curtains, after which
she cackled hilariously. This is all I know for certain
about my grandfather: 1) his name was Olshevski,
and he changed it shortly after his marriage,
when they were living in an Irish neighborhood,
2) while working at Con Ed he bought a yacht
my grandmother said, but my mother said "Mom,
it was just a boat," 3) he left Katherina
after the fourth son was born, and she lived
in a tiny apartment on Chauncy Street
which smelled, even when I was eight,
like boiled diapers, 4) he was reported
to be handsome and have "a roving eye,"
5) my father and his brothers
all of whom are dead now
refused to go to his funeral
and never spoke of him.

This is a poem about forgiving Grandpa
for my not knowing him. And father, if you're
reading over my shoulder, I don't forget how
you had three cents spending money a week

and gave two cents to the church, or how
Uncle George, the baby who was everybody's
darling, couldn't go to college because he had
to work to support the family like everybody else
and how he became a fire chief in the City of New York,
and how Uncle Will, before he died of cancer,
became an advisor to La Guardia and made a bundle
by being appointed trustee of orphans' estates,
or how Uncle Frank, driving his battery truck
once was stopped by Will and La Guardia in their big car
and they chatted, and Uncle Frank — my favorite uncle,
neither Olshevski nor Ochester — still talks
about how his partner Paddy kept saying
"Bejasus, it was the Mayor,"
or how, because you had to support your brothers,
you couldn't marry till 30
and were engaged for eight years to my mother
who to this day loves you because you did
what you had to do, and how you built your business
going door-to-door selling insurance on Chauncy Street
and Myrtle Avenue till late at night, arguing and collecting
quarters and dimes from people who lived in tiny apartments
smelling of boiled diapers.
Nearly twenty years since your death, father,
and long ago I've forgiven you, and I think
you did love me really, and who am I, who was born
as you said "with everything," to condemn
your bitterness toward your father who left you
with nothing?

I don't believe in original sin.
I believe if we're strong enough and gather our powers
we could work it out: no petty human misery,
no windrows of the dead slaughtered
in suicide charges, no hearts shrunken
and blackened like meat spitted
and held too long to the fire.
But what everybody knows
is enough to make you laugh
and to break your heart.
Grandpa, forty years after your death,
by the power vested in me as the oldest
living Ochester in the direct line I hereby
forgive you. And though you died,
my mother says, penniless and alone
with no one to talk to
I hope that when you abandoned your family

you lived well. I hope you sailed your 15-foot
yacht out into Long Island Sound
with a pretty woman on board and a bottle
of plum brandy. I hope that when the huge yacht
with "Jerko II" on the stern sailed by
you looked up and said "honey,
you'll be sailing one like that some day"
and that she giggled and said "yeah,
hon, gimme a kiss" and afterward tilted
the bottle, and that the sun was shining
on the Sound, and that you enjoyed
the bitter smell of the brine and
the brilliance of the white scud and
that when you made love that night
it was good and lasted
a long, long time.

WEEHAWKEN FERRY

The bulletnosed cars lined up behind
the bluntnosed cars; the men who
cast the hawsers off were redfaced
in the cold and spat and spat. Goodbye
New York. Everybody wore fedoras or
little pill hats with feathers. Hello
Jersey. Always in the river clots
of brown foam, orange peels, rotted wood
chipped from the spongy piers. Green
paint chipping off rails, over there
the green woman with the torch. Huge
sexual trembling of the screws positioning
the hulk in its slip. Motors coughing on,
and the slow crawl past bills: Ray
Bolger, Charlie's Aunt, Oklahoma, Ike,
Ike, Ike, Ike, Ike, and the old car
climbed the switchback carved
into the lordly Hudson's Palisades,
slipping on the cobbles and the brown ice.
At the crest the Sunday stillness of
gray frames, Ike, Ike, here and there
a new pair of shoes with leather soles
and heels walked slowly the iced sidewalks.

DIET

Just a bit
is enough. A few
slices of pak choi
limp in pale broth,
watery squash and
fresh tomatoes.
In the Depression
my father was bone
and dream, the air
so thin he saw clearly.
One could live a year
on an image:
his Clark Gable mustache
scratched out by
straight razor; him,
as he raised the walls
of his home,
polishing each
heavy cobble.

THE CANARIES IN UNCLE ARTHUR'S BASEMENT

In the white house in Rutherford
the ancient upright piano never worked
and the icy kitchen smelled of Spic 'N Span.
Aunt Lizzie's pumpkin pie turned out green
and no one ate it but me and I did
because it was the green of the back porch.
That was the Thanksgiving it rained and I first thought
of rain as tears, because Aunt Lizzie was in tears
because Arthur came home from the soccer game drunk
and because he missed dinner brought a potted plant
for each female relative, and walked around the table
kissing each one as Lizzie said "Arthur, you
fool, you fool," the tears running down her cheek as
Arthur's knobby knees wobbled in his referee's
shorts, and his black-striped filthy shirt wet from the rain
looked like a convict's. What did I know?
I thought it meant something. I thought
no one would ever be happy again. I thought
if I were Uncle Arthur I'd never again
come out from the dark basement where he raised canaries,
the cages wrapped in covers Aunt Lizzie sewed,
and where, once, when I was very small and because Uncle
    Arthur
loved me or loved his skill or both he slowly removed the cover
from a cage and a brilliant gold bird burst into song.

THREE WHITE KIDS SINGING DOO-WOP

What did I ever need besides
my blue modified pegged pants
with the white saddle stitches and
a skinny black belt, and Bobby Tarantino,
the drummer, with his black boots with the real
sharp spic heels, and George Cava in pants
so tight he needed "a shoehorn to get into them,"
waiting in the sunlight in spring
in front of the Bohack store
on Myrtle Avenue for the bus
to take us to school, while we do little shuffle
steps and dips and sing in the strong sun?
What does anybody really need?

Doo-wop a bam sham boom sha bam.

WORKING AT THE WHOLESALE CURTAIN SHOWROOM

"Can you type?" Jake said.
"Maybe ten words a minute."
"That's OK," Jake said, "we just get
a couple letters now and then,
what we need is a smart kid to be nice
to customers, you don't have to know nothin
about curtains, just be nice when people
come through the door, talk nice to the buyers
you don't have to know nothin about curtains,
just show them the way to the samples,
we got all the stuff, the styles, the prices,
printed on the cards. What we need is a nice
educated kid, like you, you'll do fine."

And I did, and this is in praise of Jake,
may he have prospered, who payed me for nothing,
and who knew the great secret of living:
"be nice," and who once sent me with roses
to the apartment of a female buyer
with the warning "this is a fine lady,
look around and tell me what the place
looks like, you can tell a lot about people
from the look of their place," and I came back
and said "she's got a nice place, and she's really
pretty, and she's got a full set of the Yale Shakespeare
books in her living room," and Jake said, "oh shit,
I'll never get anywhere with her
if she's an intellectual."

HARVEY'S ASS

What he liked about the Stones' "Sweet Virginia"
was "got to scrape the shit right off your shoes"
and he'd wiggle his ass like Jagger which was
unfortunate since though Jagger's ass has been
called in print "two collar buttons" and
"a knife-edged ass" when I heard
Harvey mumble "right offf yr
shoes" I'd see his rear
swing like a monstrous
clapper without a bell,
like two pillows in pants,
like a pair of fleshy
wrecking balls in
dissynchronous dance but
that was a long time ago and he might
be dead by now, or a Libertarian, or addicted
to the Southhampton Diet, and hey at least
he heard some music
and he moved.

DUKE

It took him years to get out of the mailroom
at Whitehead Metals but he did it,
made 70 bucks a week in posting,
and though he finally got his figures neat
he always had trouble remembering which was sheet and
which was slab, and confused the ID's of pipe with OD's,
and sometimes stared at the numbers on the PO's
in his ham fists for minutes before
he subtracted the poundage from the cards.

One day when the boss was out Jackie Olson yelled
"Hey — Duke took the Mrs. to a movie last night,
The Ten Commandments. How'd you like it Duke?
D'ja understand what it was about?"
And we waited while Duke turned his huge head
like a buffalo with its horns down and said
"yeah, I liked it, it was about
the beginnin of the Catlic religion,
up yours."

THE BOSS

was a swivelchair of flab slowly sucking
smoke from a corncob who wanted respect,
who wanted to be called "Mr. Ciccatano"
or "Boss," which he probably would have been
if his long protruding lips hadn't resembled
Dopey's in *Snow White*, and when the older guys
called him "Sam" he pretended not to hear,
though it wasn't just his looks but that
when Mr. Grover, the Big Boss, staggered
back from lunch at 2:00 the Boss stood
to attention as though the flag,
drenched in martinis, was going by,
and the anthem in the background
was muffled giggles and some sucking noises
which he pretended not to hear but
sat down to stare into space and dream,
his pipe sending up periodic smoke clouds
as monuments to ambition, and
every afternoon he straightened
his tie in the john, put on
his sharkskin jacket and
walked out alone.
Duke swore the Boss
went once a week to the hookers on Bleecker,
and that must have cost him too, forced
to hock whatever dignity he had left
in the tiny pawnshop of the groin.

THE WHITEHEAD METALS STICKBALL TEAM AT LUNCH HOUR ON W. 10TH ST.

Duke, like a gorilla
with a stripped branch in his hand,
tongue stretching in concentration to his nose
could hit the Spauldeen pinkball into the Hudson.
Harry the Head, the nervous macrocephalic
who was your friend forever if
you bought him a shot of Cutty Sark,
was a scooter but had lousy hands.
And Jackie Olson the Ivy Leaguer
who took one course a term at night
at Columbia, played wearing one
of his three or four ties from Chipp's,
and Ronald from the warehouse
led the cheers — "le's see you fuckers
hit the ball for once" — and Tony Sciotto
who had five kids and $70 a week laughed,
always, when he ran the bases.

Thomas said "it all happens
in a flash of light," that's right
and whenever I remember those words
I think of a baseball field in August, a few gulls
floating over the bright green
as Parker hits a grand slam against LA,
or that poor street where nothing ever happened
except trucks hauling sheet and slab and
at lunch that motion and yelling
everyone in a momentary pure relation
with everybody else, and the filthy river's
gulls floating over, the joy of movement
as the sun looks down on the poor and the great
as it did on the soldiers crawling up the beach at Anzio
or on the Enola Gay in the serene
dozing its way to Hiroshima
or on the great Emperor Maximin, killed
in his tent by his troops, in June.

We're godlike in our capacity to forget.
Hey listen, once it happens, it's gone.
And don't kid yourself, when you're happy you're happy.
Don't kid yourself, when you're dead you're dead.

I don't know what happened to any of them.
I remember Jackie Olson, the smart one, was promoted
to salesman, and I remember him rigid with happiness,
bouncing up and down in his swivel chair.
The night before Harry the Head joined the army
I bought him a Scotch at the White Horse;
he got in just in time for Vietnam.

There's so much pain you're a fool
for talking about it. But what's amazing
is how those in pain think it's normal.
What's wonderful is that it never changes:
how the damned laugh and sing when they can,
how the years change everything to gold.

THE RELATIVES

Holidays, I'd look out the window for them
gathering like a flock of black-coated birds:
at Christmas, Fat Charlie, all red-faced and boozy,
he who always told jokes about outhouses and
parted his sparse hair down the middle;
crippled Marie, who didn't want to be a bother,
and Uncle George, the fierce fire chief and
Evelyn Number One with her warbling voice;
Lotte of the high Hungarian cheekbones,
who was beautiful and pious, and Uncle Arthur,
who did not always know where he was but is
the only one left of the old ones, 94 this week.

I want to name them all before they go utterly,
young women with gold at their breasts,
the men in their pride and small schemings,
songs after drink and the gossip,
old stories late into the night
as they praised their dead
as best they could, absolving
themselves with their repetitions
for never having had adequate words,
becoming thus, though clumsy,
like the *scop* in the meadhall,
like Nestor in the Pylian camp,
rescuing something from death, for the young,
for me, eating cakes with ginger ale,
listening, and it was all new:
the immigrants sailing in steerage to the New World —
"the ocean is big" my grandmother said,
who spent her whole life washing clothes —
the German builder of the bakery in Kingston,
the Wife Who Died From Grief When Her Husband Died,
the Son Who Supported His Mother and Three Brothers.

I never understood their sadness, I felt
a generation too late, at the edge of the world,
and when they left and walked out into the black
and under the street lamps on Woodhaven Blvd.
it was as though they were walking through spotlights
the way Jimmy Durante did on television
at the end of the program slowly walking,

his back bent, from spotlight to spotlight
stopping at each to turn and wave and
walk again into an infinite regression
of lights, turning and waving,
kissing goodbye.

All I have left for my children
who never knew them are a few stories
and an image of a long parade,
George and Sybil, Charles, Ernest
who always smelled of kerosene,
little people joining the famous
in shrinking as they go backward
through the abyss with the others,
older, all traveling: Ruprecht,
Harthacnut, Wang-Wei, and before them,
Arzes, Sextus Marcius, waving and bowing,
Praxithea, Agathocles, an immense crowd
kissing and walking away
until each is tiny as
one neuron or gone.

III

CONVERSATION WITH ARTUR SCHNABEL

John Cage sucks
though we mustn't say so.
When I first heard "prepared piano"
I thought of deveined liver —
little slices squeezed into the strings —
or prepared mustard, little red flags
of French's waving us on toward tiny thrills:
"Oh, Edna, I think I'm going to throw up."
At least Telemann and Neil Young aren't
entirely predictable. Ever since the war
Charles Ives makes me ill with his collages,
the little white towns in Vermont
with their orange autumn obbligatos,
the uniformed band blowing snatches
of military marches as above it all
my chopper leans over for the strafe run.
The found poem's a hundred years old
and tv quick-cuts better than Eliot.
The only thing I don't get tired of
is the heart, the way it moves
down the highway like a '47 Hudson,
that tanklike car, the tires massive
and the radio blaring, as it was years ago
when my parents drove into the great night
of upstate New York, my erection
in the back seat uncontrollable,
though I couldn't say so,
my lights flashing, all my flags flying
toward the wars.
Of course
we like "the great control"
of art because ordinarily we're hapless,
all our thrills to come,
like the redneck soldier stumbling
through Times Square, dressed to kill
with his Purple Heart on.

WALKING AROUND THE FARM

This is where I shot the rabbit
from the back porch
when we first moved in
but found it inedible,
covered with fleas. This
is where we made love
in the woods, surrounded by ferns,
our asses bitten by mosquitoes.
This is where our daughter, age six,
was tossed like a tenpin
by a running bulldog.
This is the black walnut tree
beneath which we drank beer
the morning Nixon resigned.
This is where years ago
I grew reefer among the corn.
This is the gravestone
so weathered we can't read the name.
This is where Roger parked
his Volkswagen the night he came back
from Vietnam and we listened
to Van Morrison in the rain
all night delicately sipping Jim Beam.
This is where the crabapple tree fell
during the great wind of '79.
This is the mailbox
where the postman, Mr. John,
picks up his two dozen eggs a week.
This is where we picked the lambsquarters
that sustained us in our first year.
That's where I sit in good weather
when I'm thinking a poem.
That is the road that runs
into the black woods
where my daughter, age 12,
saw something running through the brush
that she said seemed almost human, but huge,
naked and terrified.

CONVERSATION ON LADY DAY

The daffodil is not like a trumpet
but an old stand-up telephone.
I can talk into it
and the roots will transmit
by gathering the voice
into the big base bulb
and pulse it through
tiny neurotransmitters
in the hair roots.
"Hello, hello."
I can never hear anything
but I'll talk:
a year ago we sat at the table
under the tree and drank wine
beneath the Pleiades shower.
They weren't stars, but they were falling.
Do you remember making inspections
of the garden? Counting the kohlrabi,
dressing up the garlic,
how you were followed by the cats?
We're all going into the dark forever.
The animals just want us to love them.
We're not too different.
If you hear this
will you retransmit?
When someone talks into the bell of a daffodil
he expects nothing if not a miracle.
Which is always there:
the cats picking their careful ways
among the young onions,
the red leaves on the maples,
you in the distance, waving.

THE COIN DREAM

Betsy said "in my dream
there was a huge pool of water
in the back yard and I was diving
for coins, there were coins everywhere
and whenever I dove I found beautiful ones,
old Greek coins with swans and doves.
Ned found a coin that you said was rare
and priceless, but whenever I dove
I found coins you said were beautiful
and that you would always treasure.
That dream was so real I still know
where I found the most wonderful ones,
under the big maple root
near the clothesline. There was one
with a lady in a helmet
holding a spear and a shield
that looked like the moon. Tomorrow
I'm going out there to see if the dream
was telling me something."
And I said "it was."

POEM FOR A NEW CAT

Watching her stand on the first
joints of her hind legs like a kangaroo
peering over the edge of the bathtub
at my privates floating like a fungoid lilypad,
or her bouncy joy in pouncing on a crumpled
Pall Mall pack, or the way she wobbles walking
the back of the couch, I think when
was it we grew tired of everything?
Imagine the cat jogging, terrified
that her ass might droop, or studying
the effective annual interest paid
by the First Variable Rate Fund, the cat
feeling obliged to read those poems that
concentrate the sweetness of life like prunes.
O.K., that's ridiculous — though the cat
also kills for pleasure — but I find
myself in the middle of the way,
half the minutes of my sentient life
told out for greed and fear.
The cat's whiskers are covered with lint
from the back of the dryer.
      Friend,
how it is with you I don't know
but I'm too old to die.

THE LATIN AMERICAN SOLIDARITY COMMITTEE FUNDRAISING PICNIC

"What we'd like to do," he said
"is include some local poets
in the entertainment."
"Sure," I said.
It was at the Mellon Pavilion
in Frick Park and when I got there
they were running late. "Listen,"
he said, "I"m really sorry,
the poetry has to go later in the program
because we still haven't raffled off
the bottle of Cuban rum."
"Sure," I said.
After the Cuban rum there was an interlude
with mariachi music and solo guitar and
then a professor of sociology
gave a full account of his recent
trip to Cuba and how the Cuban people
despite having just broken the ubiquitous
chains of American economic exploitation
showed unfailing courtesy to visiting dignitaries
such as himself.
By this time it was almost dark.
"Jeez," he said, "if we have the poetry now
we'll never get in any volleyball."
"That's ok," I said, "I like volleyball."
So I played, and the other team was pretty good,
I got three balls spiked in my face.
After that I drank some beer and talked
with a pretty Mexican woman.
After the beer ran out I went home.
Under the cover of darkness
the revolution was gathering steam.

THE HISTORIAN'S WIDOW

"We're mostly echoes of the past"
he said. He knew them all from Caesar
to Romulus Augustulus and Zeno and
if he were drinking, at a party say,
never much but he'd do it, he'd name them
all so that I learned some and I remember
once *in bed*: "Vespasian, Titus, Domitian,
Nerva, Trajan, Hadrian, Antoninus Pius."
"The past is clearer than the present,"
that's true, don't you think? Once
he got the professorship at London it was
easier — good flat, the Mediterranean and
he loved recipes of Apicius: origany,
dry mint, lovage, raisin wine, white beets,
Damascus plums, and also coins: denarii,
sesterce, antoniniani, in their wooden
cabinet all the emperors and their ladies
in that little box, Roma, Fortuna,
Venus, nude, holding out an apple,
Faustina Junior, Julia Domna, Lavinia,
he particularly loved the ladies,
a carpenter form Livorno made it,
he kept them all in there.

POEM FOR BASHO

If I am timorous and
hestitant to intrude
on your privacy,

forgive me, for though
every poet in New York
has written a poem to you

it is different here
where one farm does not wish
to violate another

farm's solitude, but
if after 300 years you
were here in this valley

perhaps you would write
about the mouse who
every night travels out

to eat at the dog's dish.
And I think you would like
the wind stunted spruce

and the way the drip, drip
of the sink gathers
the night around it.

Basho, here is my yellow glass.
I am alone, but happy because
I do not have to be alone.

You understood that, surely?
How one of the pleasures
of silence is finally

returning to your friends.
Even though, no doubt, they thought
you slightly peculiar.

What are the colors of flowers
at night? And Basho, will you

have another glass of rice wine

or whiskey? Basho, may
I show you a poem I've just written?
Basho, what are 300 years?

ABANDONED FARM, KITTATINNY

Plenty of water at the spring
if you take it slow, enough anyway
to drink. Maybe they left this place
because the spring grudges waste,
and there wasn't enough
for flushing stables or
watering an automated barn.
"Goddam" they said one day
and left, a pair of dirty
blue jeans on the floor.

But it's enough for two lovers
passing through. They could drink
and come back after a while
and find the water fresh
and sweet and cold.

MARY MIHALIK

She'd tried to kill herself before.
Six kids, no money.

She was drunk
they said, doing 80, 90

on the slick blacktop
twisty and at dusk, and they

said there were no skidmarks
where she sailed under

the coal truck going slow
uphill out of the crossroad and

sheared the top of her Chevette
clean off and the rumor was

that when the cops came,
in the back seat they found her head.

People said all she needed
was a job, and I guess they're right.

And probably everyone thought
she needed love but everybody

says you've got to earn that,
though I think love's a gift,

the way money is for some, who
have a lot and never earned it.

I don't know. But a few nights later
when I walked past there, the insects

were at their cheerful static.
Aside from them the woods were silent.

And there were fireflies.

NEW DAY

Yes, the sun rises an angry red,
what the Romans called *oriens*,
what the religious associate with Christ,
and I walk out in my shorts, stretching
and puffing to train the scarlet runner beans
to their trellis; whatever god governs
beans has smiled, the vines grown
a foot overnight, and as I lace them
around the nervous network of twine
my son, who last night collapsed
in an anguish of stertorous breathing
comes down, stretches and yawns, pees.
Pots rattle in the kitchen,
grits and eggs,
and the rooster with a pneumonic lung
croaks — oohgggHHH — for the sun
but he hasn't died yet and
as I'm eating, the radio says
the President is lobbying
to subvert another small country
and I flip the dial and a preacher
who knows nothing says that except
for one thing there is nothing to know,
and when I walk out again
a hummingbird's in the salvia,
the sun's up, the dog on his chain
whines for breakfast, and the squash
are flourishing and when I stand near them
with my bright yellow shirt the cucumber beetles,
who love anything yellow, land on me and
are destroyed, sinners on the shirt
of a jealous god, and the sun's rising
to zenith, the chickens are scratching
around in their mud and if you
were very young you could say
this is heaven what with the dew
and the birds chirpy and all and yes
if you wait long enough
you will see the new moon
with the old moon in her arms.

POEM WRITTEN FOR THE FIFTH ANNIVERSARY OF THE THREE RIVERS SHAKESPEARE FESTIVAL

The thing he knew most about us was that we dream
our lives, until pain or love awaken us, and so
in this theater we are most alive. Sometimes,
when the play is over and I walk out onto Forbes,
back into the little O of our world,

I think of the great Elizabeth, of her young court
compact of music, dance and more lovers
than Belmont held, how finally the music fled and,
her heart halting, in late age she killed her last
lover, Essex; the lonely queen in an absurd red wig;

and I watch the lovers walking down Forbes at night
to their own unexpected destinies, and the solitary
figures rapidly going somewhere, and the lights of the city,
and I know that the certainties in our tentative hearts
are upheld by words alone, as for instance Portia, who

by her hard gaiety holds the whole rotten edifice
of Venice up. After the play I want to talk to friends,
I want to be a part again of the bright coming and going

in the dark, as Shakespeare was in his great city,
which is ours, with the same eternal gossip of the heart,
the same characters walking the long streets,

the same miracle of some humans dreaming
"not the smallest orb which thou behold'st
but in his motion like an angel sings."

BLIZZARD, DECEMBER 2

My son calls to say his plane arrived
safely in Chicago and he's in his overheated room

but on tv I see Green Bay playing in a blizzard
that's moving east, the first flakes perhaps

hissing in the Chicago River, swirling around
the Art Institute blacked out on a Sunday night,

then moving into Indiana, smothering the motel
in Valparaiso where a quarter century ago

I made love to a girl I hardly knew and later
we both cried in the bar at the thought of parting

because at that age one is the most romantic
or stupid, because one wants to be

and everything should last, including
the pretty illusions of permanence,

and now the snow is covering the great dead
U. S. Steel works at Gary and gathering itself

in fury to cover the tiny hills, small as
burial mounds, around Elkhart where last summer

I had dinner in a good place with fresh oysters
when I was dead tired and the waitress

asked if I knew how Captain Hook had died
— *"crotch itch!"* she said, roaring — and then the snow

with nothing to stop it whistles into Ohio
and the Turnpike shuts down except for the plows

with their eerie lights flashing cruising the wastes
and Cleveland goes under and I hope Bob Wallace

is safe and warm and has plenty of brandy
for his Alexanders and the storm descends

on Akron where Elton is still a little melancholy
again for not getting the job back home in New Orleans

and then into the foothills of the Alleghenies
and in Pittsburgh the travellers coming in

from the airport will exit the tunnel above downtown
and see the first flakes settling and the beautiful lights

and say "shit" and prepare to slide down the terrible hills
as always and I hope all of my friends are home

looking out at the night as the huge flakes
descend, as they say on tv, "in earnest,"

and not out on the black streets with the cars
slipping sideways, and the snow moves east

and begins to coat our country roads and
the township's two-man road crew say

"damn" at midnight and get up and begin
to cruise the dirt roads with their twenty

year old plow, and kids have been staring at snow
against the barn lights and hoping no school for a week and

not thinking about all the natural associations
of snow with death and separation or how

in the morning the snow will be a foot deep
on the bales of hay covering the carrots

in the garden, the golden spikes shrinking
from the cold the way that the penises

even of football players do, and it is
the season of death, though if everyone you love

is ok and the smoke curls from the lost chimneys
of houses in the next valley you can bear it,

and tomorrow morning, the first day of deer season,
I will be out on the porch sniffing the air

and grumbling, and go inside where my books
are sleeping on their shelves, and my guns

are sleeping on their racks because I don't
hunt now, though outside men are rejoicing

because you can track a wounded deer
by its trail of blood in the snow, but

what I'm thinking most is that my son
is walking around as they dig out in Chicago

and that everything is safe again in the deep earth
and that nothing is the system right now can hurt us.

FOR THE ZOROASTRIANS

"the religion was concerned...with protecting
and treating kindly domestic animals"
--*The New Columbia Encyclopedia*

Nietzsche, who knew a thing or two,
preferred *Zarathustra*, as closer to the Persian,
though either way the name means "camel handler"
and I prefer to think of Zoroaster
as an early version of St. Francis working
with people equally thick skulled
to whom he said "friend, if you will refrain
from incessantly punching your cow
it may give more milk," or "honey,
if you want more eggs, stop
twirling your chickens by their tails,"
and since his wisdom was practical
as well as spiritual the Persians adopted
Zoroastrianism as the state religion and
the Sassanian dynasty put a fire altar
on the back of all its coins —
not that the Zoroastrians worshiped fire,
they just saw its purity as manifestation
of God, or Mazdah — and all their emperors,
whose names sound like Tolkien made them up,
Ardashir and Sapur and Yazdgard and Xusro,
ruled in the golden city of Zoroastrian light,
Ctesiphon, where flutes played erotic music
and the great merchants presided over banquets
where the most desirable women in the world
sang their learned poetry, their dear nipples rouged,
which now are dust, the emperors fled, vanished,
when the great horde of Allah,
the "horse people" Zoroaster feared who
need to subjugate and move on endlessly
burned the city with its famous towers
and blue fountains in the desert
all in the name of God

and only a few refugees reached India
where they became the Parsees of Bombay
who have "economic importance far greater
than their small numbers would indicate,"
and the encyclopedia names the great industrial
family of the Tatas — strange,
because the eldest Tata son, Ratan,

was my classmate at Cornell, he
with his soft eyes liquid as an animal's
who could assume the lotus position
and walk up stairs on his knees;
nor does the strangeness of their belief bother me:
Zoroaster's, that the world would endure just
12,000 years from the creation, or the Parsees'
exposure of their dead in "towers of silence"
for the vultures to devour, though we
know better, of course, and smile at anything,
for example the statue of the many-breasted Diana
at Ephesus, long ago destroyed by war, or the Manichees
who believed like Zoroaster that Satan was outside
the Power of God, and that the forces of the great light
and the great darkness were joined in equal battle,
and I believe,.as did my catechizer, Pastor Hucke —
he who was so enthused playing
"A Mighty Fortress Is Our God"
that he once fell off his stool —
that it's heresy to believe wine is really turned to blood
though I remember the ladies of our church
dicing Wonder Bread into little cubes
("builds strong bodies eight ways")
to represent the body of our Lord.

I'm sitting in an old farmhouse in the dark
late at night, and I too fear the horse people,
the President mad with good will and power,
old, blind and idiotic, who lines the missiles up.
Maybe because of Zoroaster
I scratch the bulldog's ears, and give him
a bit more of the liver and onions that he wants.
Bless the creatures. Bless us all in our absurdities.
I thank the distant and disinterested Ochester god
for Vivaldi, for physical love, for life, even
the loaf of Generic Wheat Bread my son has just devoured.
Given the small progress that we ever make I swear
I'll fix the chickens' leaking roof, and
I forgive the Pope his seven Rolls-Royces and
I'm happy that the Vatican is in the process
of forgiving Galileo for saying that the earth
revolves around the great fire after,
lord, only these 400 years.

IV

THE MUSE

Quite a few of them, actually,
academic muses who are the sisters of Morpheus,
and the Medusa Muse who looks like *Il Duce*
and trades in various manifestations of hate, and
The New Yorker Muse, who is notoriously
dipsomaniacal and dances around on little
mouse feet, but my muse is a single mother
traveling north with a carful of kids,
she sends a postcard to say
"still feeling sorry for yourself, wimp-o?"
My muse was the first muse to hide
her stash behind a loose ceiling tile
in Ithaca, New York, and had the lowest recorded
average for a graduating senior, my muse
got married in the nude to a bartender
in the woods and regretted it shortly
afterward. My muse
knew Big Bill Haywood.
My muse has been keeping ten cats
in a small apartment and is slow
to change the litter. My muse
reads Brecht and sometimes pretends
she's Lotte Lenya; just when I think
she's settling down she shows up
with one immense Mona Lisa earring.
Once, on the rock hill in back of my house,
she said: "Look, give it up, all you know
is that if you're any good maybe you'll know more
tomorrow, and why shouldn't you wear
your heart on your sleeve, in your case
it needs fresh air, and as for form,
O'Hara was right, if you're buying jeans
you might as well get them tight
as possible you can kiss me now."

O muse, come back, I'm lonely and pedestrian,
I'm reading *USA Today*, and I'm afraid
and feel powerless and there's Reagan
and his undeclared wars

Ο ΠΡΟΚΤΟΣ
how many times

*must i tell you
whatever blossoms
is rooted in the dark.*

THE HEART OF OWL COUNTRY

Whatever blossoms is rooted
in the dark as, item

the delicate purple comfrey flower
supported by a brutish taproot

that powers itself into the subsoil
and splits the shale a dozen feet

beneath me, so that the bumblebees
tumble in a drunken frenzy here, and

item, how if I tend my loneliness,
which is no rarer than yours,

friend, I grow stronger,
so that my fists open, and the garden

becomes a natural metaphor for what
we have always known:

that only by going deeply
as possible into our dark

can we discover ourselves
to others, and even though

the stutterer I have always been
would like to say "we will never

die" I know that we will utterly
except for what we yield to friends

or progeny — that's the garden part —
and I remember now what I'd forgotten

for years, how, once, when we were
driving to my mother's, in New York State,

at twilight passing through a large marsh
my daughter said *look!* and in every dead

tree there was an owl, hundreds of them,
stupid in the light, like a faculty senate,

staring uncomprehendingly at the swamp
and the cars on the interstate, so still

one could have knocked them off their
perches with a stick and my daughter

screamed, delighted, "this must be
the heart of owl country!" and it
was: those soft fists of feathers
waiting for their hour, long

after we'd passed lifting into the spring air
on their solitary flights, each silent

in its large community, alert and perfect.

POEM ON HIS 44TH BIRTHDAY

After so many years I've discovered
what my family taught me, they
who never saw gill-over-the-ground
or at least could not name it.
My mother was thinking in the typing pool:
be like those cheerful leaves;
no matter how often you pull
or slash it the foot of its root
will venture out. In drought it
sends its small purple flowers up.
My uncle with his acid stained hands
and eaten-out sweaters must have known
driving the battery truck:
wait long enough and the stripmine will flower,
the birds will pass over and the dock plant
will root, the acid leach out
through the growing humus and grasses.
This must be why they kept flowers
in the gray house, and the dusty ivy
and indestructible snakeplants
which fried and seethed on the radiators.
Even my father, whose heart exploded
between two giant spruce he'd planted
with his pale hands years ago
must have known it, going down,
as he fell for the last time
to the earth and his fingers clawed in,
and the birds whose names he never knew
finally settled and continued
their only and endless song:
rejoice, rejoice.

SELLING BOOKS AT THE JAMES WRIGHT FESTIVAL IN MARTINS FERRY, OHIO

—"The very name of America often makes me
sick, and yet Ralph Neal was an American.
The country is enough to drive you crazy."

James Wright, "The Flying Eagles of Troop 62"

—*for Elton Glaser*

The sign said WRIGHT FESTIVAL but
the street was closed, and a hundred kids,
little ones, were shouting and crawling
around the cracked macadam, and a long-haired guy
with a bull horn was yelling at them and
another sign said HOT WHEELS and I said
"Jesus, how are we going to get to it?"
and Britt said "we'll have to carry
the books five blocks," but later

inside, drinking coffee, Annie said
"if James were here he wouldn't be inside,
he'd be out there with the children,"
and during the long afternoon, even after
the children had vanished, I kept thinking
how little I've ever understood, resigned
to that impatient stupidity imprinted
in our gene pool since my ancestors stumbled
around in the East Prussian mud, and it wasn't

until the dinner catered by Henry Lash,
who has the baggiest pants I've ever seen
and who hitches rides with his utensils and food
and said "I've never *not* got a ride," or until
a few beers at Dutch Henry's with the local
promqueens and the man with the plastic shoes
who was seriously peeing on the john wall
and said "evenin,' " or until I saw how happy
Elton was about going home to New Orleans

and heard him tell how his daddy bought crabs
and shrimp and crawfish for a boil because he
was happy too; not till then, or later, at night,
did I understand what Wright loved here,
these strange flowers of lives growing

above the oil-slicked shore, just as
in the thirties in Europe people sang
and danced and made love, and I remembered
the photo of a couple raising their hands

as if in victory, in Madrid, just before
the Civil War broke out, and I thought
as I drove over the high humpbacked bridge
into Wheeling past the Marsh-Wheeling Cigar
sign how during the early forties despite
rationing my parents held as often
as before their poor feasts and they
were lovely as the necklace of lights
yellow and white on the river that runs

through America, bloated and polluted,
imperturbably to the Gulf.

ROCK HILL

Standing midway on the rock hill,
thinking of the sea, I want to gesticulate
and be theatrical, I want to shout
Thalassa, Thalassa to name her because
I remember how, years ago, we floated
like a pod of whales, massive and
oblivious, in the chop off Truro,
smoking cigars in the sea
as our friends watched and
neither the audacity of the waters
nor the idiocy of youth mattered
to what we were, white paddlers
asserting ourselves, drifting
into our futures with the cigars
fuming like steamships.
                But
here on the rock hill I want
more than my old story I want not just
gesture, but particular, not *me* but me
among the articulations of the creatures,
the hummingbird searching the beanflowers,
its iridescent breast big as a bumblebee,
the corn dropping pollen in sunlight
and moonlight, what I forget till I walk here,
the other dim lives suffering this world
and glorying in it, the intelligent
imprinted roots of the squash vines &
the vines sprawling through and around the corn,
the carrots with their sexual thrust
and stolidity.
              A cat arches her back
in the sun and dares me to speak.
"A tiny beetle with six dots on its shell
labors over a pebble, a green tomato worm
the size and shape of my thumb is going
deathward, its back bristling with white
parasite eggs." This poem is never going
to end, me here with my memories and this
fresh world, and the children distant in the house
their lovely youth making them immortal
as the sea slaps their bodies
and the sun sails by.

HAVING BUILT THE COOP

"for centuries I have been forced
to sleepwalk on these roads of decay"
—d.a.levy, "The North American
Book of the Dead"

I put the chickens in and they swivel
their necks, tentative, suspicious,
their merciless unblinking eyes
reminders that they descended
from reptiles, though these are loveable
as they coo and cluck and their behinds
wiggle as they settle down to turn
the tiny compound into a mud flat
and then don't even try to escape,
though the grass they love is growing
luxuriantly a few inches beyond
the woven wire fence, because the coop
is home and from my point of view
I want their eggs in one place
even though it's the nature of chickens
insofar as one can talk about "nature"
to be pecking through a broad universe
of an acre or more, and I suppose
the moral, if there is a "moral,"
is what levy said: it's all illusion,
but you may as well follow your own
as the illusions of others — though the chickens
don't care, the chickens cackle over some
culled spinach they adore and a handful
of cracked corn and cluck "this is
the best place in the world" though
of course they haven't been to any other
because they're in a cage but that's ok,
they don't live too long and they're
never going to read Thucydides or
hit many good restaurants, they
are there to work, and it amazes me
how intelligent levy was for someone
who died at 23 but still understood
that "everyone pays their dues
& no one's gettin' the product"
though that was twenty years back
and none of the chickens are complaining
this June as the invisible cicadas sing
derrida • derrida • derrida

THANKSGIVING

On the tube, the old parade:
they've shoveled the shit off the streets
to make room for the starlets and
Conan the Barbarian with that tight helmet
to keep his skull screwed down and
His Eminence the Archbishop of N.Y.
waves as though to say "howdy folks,
I hope you're not contemplating
an abortion" and the Arkansas Razorback
Marching Band plays some of Mozart's
greatest hits from *Amadeus* and the sun
blesses everything like a kid
watching tv with one eye
on his homework and

I see myself there in a brown snowsuit
with a zippered hood, waving
a diminutive flag above the crowd
and yelling to my father "higher!
hold me higher!" in front of an automat
where I learned later bums & kids went
for free lemonade, got lemon wedges
from the condiment trays and sugar
to mix with free ice at the water cooler —
one of the few mercies the city provided
but stopped giving long since — and
to which my father took me for years
for his favorite restaurant meal,
automat beans, baked in little brown pots
with a thin glaze of pork grease on top
and explained, always, that there was no
other city in the world where you could put
quarters and nickels in a slot and
get a pot of beans like that and

here's a band from Williamsport, PA —
"a town that's more that just Little League"
says Bobby Arnold the MC, who played
a corpse on V — doing its "unique" rendition
of "Stardust" beneath the world's first and largest
floating rubberized deconstructionist critic
masquerading as the Michelin Man and as far

as I can see this thing goes on forever,
dwarfs and Prince and minimum wage teens
carrying buckets and brooms behind
the Aleppo Shrine Horse Patrol and Placido Domingo
("hey man, don't step in the Placido Domingo!")

LOVE POEM WITH BOMB

Didn't Pius VIII say
"every new Christian brings us
a bit closer to Armageddon"?
Maybe we should all read Aristotle's
Rhetoric again, though it may
be too late in the day for that
since the barbarians are not
only at the gates but collecting
the tolls; hardly anyone knows
that Carlos Williams proposed
but O'Hara delivered, and let's face it:
if you concentrate your energies
on killing you don't have time
to learn why you shouldn't kill,
like the colonel in 'Nam who said
"the trouble with you guys is
you'd rather fuck than fight"
(wouldn't you?)

Nostradamus said: "Beware
the country that publishes
the most self-help books,"
but because I don't understand him
myself, I have to face the possibility
we'll survive; either way
I'll go down with you.
The giant oak I see from the bathroom
is slowly unfurling its leaves like
it means to hang around, and at night
the fat moths bounce off the glass.
For millenia we've been holding hands
in the dark again and again.

APRIL, NEAR THE SCHOOL FOR THE BLIND

I come up to
a column of blind children,
two by two, holding hands,
led by their teacher,
out for a walk in the sun
and four have fallen behind,
stalled at a garden where one
has picked a crocus and
is tearing at it with his teeth,
tasting crocus, delicately,
chewing and tasting, and
the teacher halts the group
and runs back to yell
what are you doing?
will you please
tell me what you're doing?

THE ODDS

Over the phone I say "look,
if you want something to say
about Levine say that in contrast
to the clear certainty of Wilbur
his poems are about how hard
it is to know the past or capture
the present, and if you want
something to talk about
talk about entropy in, say,
Pynchon and Levine, you know?"
and after I put the receiver
down I stare at the Roman ring
on the skinny fourth finger
of my left hand, how the etching
in the bronze fabric may be
a flower or, upside down,
a penis with large testicles
and lots of flowery
pubic hair and then I
walk over to the Music Bldg.
because Wayne Slawson
has roped me into
a Ph.D. committee
though I know nothing about
the "tone colours" the student
has written on because I
was chosen to help with the
Roethke text he set to music
but he's pulled a fast one and
not written on Roethke but on
Subsets of the Eight Colour Collection
and so I say "you really shouldn't
leave Roethke out of your bibliography"
and "if you, say, publish this, you'd
better be sure to get permission
from Doubleday, maybe send
the permissions manager the text
of what you've done so he/she
doesn't think, um, you're simply
an unserious crank" and after
we shake hands, and he really
is a nice young guy who says

he's *really* happy to be moving
to Philadelphia, and the other
faculty member from Music
I don't know and who said
"hello I've heard a lot about you"
but whose name I didn't catch
says goodbye, I go back
to the Press where Amy the student
who's taking John's place is
logging in manuscripts and says
"I think I can work on these
all week if you don't need
the office" and I say "sure,
I think I'll be in, though
Wednesday afternoon" and she says
"Oh. That's when we're going
to the Pirate game after work"
and I say "yes, that was my idea
though since the Pirates dropped
four out of five to the Mets
I'm not sure I should have
suggested it, you know?
maybe they're so down
they'll blow all three games
with the Cubs, but maybe we can,
say, find some guys who still
believe in the Pirates and
maybe get gamblers' odds
anyway" and she says "yeah,
get a book on the game"
and tonight as I'm typing
the Pirates win in the top
of the 11th,
5-4.

TWO WOMEN WATCHED BY GEESE

in the lowlands, in the valley
of the Kiskiminetas: three geese,
white ones, silent and still, as the young women
stare at their chimney, or the blue November sky,
or the sun, one with her hand cupping her breast
as I drive by with boxes of books in the back seat,
Jerry Lee Lewis singing "It'll Be Me."

I wanted to tell you this, I think it may be
a love poem for the prestidigitations
of this world and for you, for the plain
secrets we stand in and sometimes give way to,
loving for once where and what we are
like those women staring at loose bricks
or God, the geese too in their dim
imprinted lives thinking "mother !" and
that's ok, let them wiggle their tails,
they only think they're happy but
they're happy. Love's in the saddle
sometimes, that dumb rider that
ties us to the earth, like a thumb rubbing
the amethyst in my pocket or the Swiss coin
I've carried for years. "Don't speak" I'd say
if you were here. Years ago I threw
the gold ring into the corn on the rock hill
and that's what I meant, I think: "be
the crop growing," though that was portentous —
it was the 70's, honey — and now I'd say, ok
love is a relative value but that's not bad
if you don't have any absolutes around and
anyway what do I have but the things of this world,
two women staring at the sun, three geese
enthralled as I ride by in the sealed car
and a mile or so down the road understand
for once and hit the horn and honk
and honk and honk.

FOR THE MARGRAVE OF
BRANDENBURG

When I'm driving up Bellefield in spring
with the window down and Bach needling
the air, Bach at the celestial sewing machine,
as the magnolia petals fall to the pavement
like fleshy coins, I think of you, and your daughters
if you had any — and you must have had them,
any uncle of the King of Prussia must have had
dozens of little dumplings dressed in silk,
and sons, all pimply in wigs, dabbling at harpsichords,
and not getting it right, poor things —
when the gift of the concerti first arrived
from Bach at Anhalt-Cothen, how your daughters
wrinkled their noses and puffed their waxed apple
cheeks, and the sons attended to their nose hairs
as the little clutch of journeymen musicians
you kept fiddled and squeaked, drops
of sweat plopping from their upper lips
as they labored over music too difficult to play
but which still said, plainly, O dumplings!
O zits! *macht auf* with the periwigs,
into the woods, the sunned air, the freshets
of vertiginous water, when you die you are dead
for so long no niceties of taffeta or toupee,
no good regard of the godful will redeem your death,
don't let my masses mislead you to studied solemnity,
serious doesn't mean solemn, necessarily, (signed:)
Papa Bach, Papa Bach, Papa Bach.

POEM FOR DR. SPOCK

I too when I die do not wish
to encumber my friends with the burdens
of sorrow: I want a simple ceremony,
twenty minutes or so, a few poems,
a brief testimonial, a tear or two
against plain black velvet and
as for the corpse burn it, scatter
the ashes around my asparagus plants,
which need large infusions of lime,
or throw them in the eyes of my enemies,
and let the mourners go off to a party,
a staid one where the waiters pour rivers
of Dom Perignon and nobody has to worry
about money for once, and later
a wild one with live music, a reappearance
of the Bonzo Dog Band, if possible, and
recapitulations of every drug popular
for the last fifty years, laughter
and solidarity for days. Let them stay
as long as they wish and then go
satiated, prepared again for the world,
and let the mouse of grief
gnaw at their hearts forever.